Louise Chandler Moulton

Evaline, Madelon, and other Poems

Louise Chandler Moulton

Evaline, Madelon, and other Poems

ISBN/EAN: 9783744711241

Printed in Europe, USA, Canada, Australia, Japan

Cover: Foto ©Thomas Meinert / pixelio.de

More available books at **www.hansebooks.com**

EVALINE, MADELON,

And other Poems.

BY

LOUISA CHANDLER.

LONDON:
JOHN BUMPUS, 158 OXFORD STREET.
1861.

TO THE

RIGHT HON. THE VISCOUNT RAYNHAM, M.P.

These Poems are Inscribed,

AS A TRIBUTE OF RESPECT TO HIS PUBLIC CHARACTER,

AND IN GRATEFUL ACKNOWLEDGMENT OF

MANY ACTS

OF PERSONAL KINDNESS.

JOHANNA CHANDLER,
EDWARD HENRY CHANDLER.

THE

SISTERS' MEMORIAL FUND,

FOR THE PARALYSED AND EPILEPTIC.

SOME few years since, two Sisters (orphans), who had been reared by their Grandmother, sat awaiting her return; she came at last, but how changed! She had left them cheerful and active,—she was carried in a helpless burden: she had been suddenly stricken with Paralysis. Always of strong and active habits, "the thing she most feared had come upon her;" the shadow deepened upon the once happy home, until it pleased God to take the poor afflicted one to Himself.

Saddened by the sufferings of one so dear, and deeply impressed with the conviction, that if those surrounded with all the comforts of life thus suffered, the condition of the Paralysed Poor must be pitiable indeed, the Sisters conceived the idea of founding a charity for the especial benefit of persons so afflicted: but they were not rich,—they knew, too, that the wealthy and benevolent were besieged with applications, and rightly judged that theirs would be cast aside. "We know a little art," said the elder Sister, "we will practise it until we have gained 200l.; we will offer that in earnest of our sincerity, and God will incline some kind heart to take up the cause." So the little fund was worked for, gained, and offered; devoted men and women were found to take up the cause; and the Hospital for the Paralysed and Epileptic was established: but the younger Sister (always delicate) lived only to see the commencement of the good work; with her dying breath she blessed it, prayed for its success, and entered into her rest.

IN MEMORY of that loving helper, the elder Sister proposes to raise a FUND to establish Three or more Pensions of Ten Pounds annually in perpetuity, the sum required to be raised by Subscription Cards. This object secured, efforts will then be made to place the Out-door Fund of the Hospital on a permanent foundation.

All hearts, yet blessed with the endearing ties of Sister and Mother, are entreated to aid in this Memorial of a Sister's and Mother's love.

For particulars and all information, address MISS CHANDLER, 153 Albany Street, Regent's Park.

This VOLUME OF POEMS is published in Aid of the Sisters' Memorial Fund.

CONTENTS.

	PAGE
EVALINE	1
MADELON	45

MISCELLANEOUS POEMS.

LEGEND OF THE UNTERSBERG	67
JOSEPHINE AT THE FOUNTAIN	72
MURMURING	76
RESIGNATION	80
THE VILLAGE SABBATH	86
THE WANDERER	90
THE OLD BARON	94
THE TALE OF A SATIN GOWN	99

CONTENTS.

	PAGE
THE CHANT OF DEATH	107
THE KING OF THE WORLD	111
THE DRESSMAKER'S DREAM	118
THE DEATH OF SCHILLER	122
GO FORTH	127
THE TRIUMPH OF FAITH	133
DEATH AT THE HALL	138
DEATH IN THE COTTAGE	140
OH! STRIKE THY HARP	142
A VISION OF DEATH AND IMMORTALITY	144
THE BURIAL OF THE EMIGRANT	150
A FACT, 1847	154
CHRISTIAN CHARITY	158

PART I.

Deep in the dusk hill's purple shade
   A valley rich in tender grace,
That pure and holy Peace had made
   Her home and dwelling-place;
The clash of storm and tempest came not there,
A brooding calm hung in the stilly air.

Dim, solemn glens were here, untrod
  By human foot — dark, waving woods,
Sacred to Nature and to God
  Their grass-grown solitudes;
Soft, timid creatures thronged their green arcades,
And loving dwelt amid their sombrous shades.

Rich meadows decked in mellow light,
  In purple heath and golden flower,—
In the long grass the daisies white
  Spread like a starry shower;
In deep and dusky dells, half hid from view
In clustered beds, the scented violets grew.

Broad beeches spread a grateful shade,
  A stream meandered at their feet;
And here the peaceful cattle strayed
  To shun the noon-day heat;
At ease reclined the mossy banks among,
The cow-boy slept, or trolled his merry song.

The village church peeped o'er the glen,
    Its walls were green with time and rot,
Five hundred years the prayers of men
    Had sanctified the spot;
The birds all loved it, and its grey roof rang
The livelong day with the glad song they sang.

The voice of waters — rushing streams —
    Adown the hills through groves unseen,
Then leaping forth in silvery gleams
    O'er slopes of richest green,
Blent with the murmurs of the soughing breeze
The bird's blithe song — the Music of the trees.

And nestling in the peaceful vale,
    There stood a thatched and lowly cot,
The blushing rose, the jasmine pale,
    Were clustered round the spot;
Here white acacia wooed the summer wind,
And fragrant woodbine all the roof entwined;

A vine its graceful beauty lent,
    And round the lattice crept and smiled;
Here dwelt in calm and deep content
    A peasant with his child;
Few of life's busy cares or joys had he,
His cottage-home — the infant at his knee —

Were all his wealth; his young wife slept
    Low in the churchyard's quiet breast,
There where the yew-trees' shadows crept
    She took her solemn rest;
Bright were the flowers around her slumbering head,
And smooth the turf that clothed her narrow bed.

And now the child was all to him,
    A little laughing, winsome thing,
Whose blue eyes made the violets dim,
    And joyous as the Spring;
For ever at his side was heard **the fleet-**
Light-rain-like patter of her tiny feet : —

EVALINE.

She danced about his steps, and thrilled
    The very air with her shrill glee,
When evening's calm his bosom filled,
    She clung around his knee;
And all night long upon his sturdy breast
Her fair head lay in sweet and trustful rest.

Sleep on in pure and blest repose
    While all around is bright and glad,
Ere o'er thee the dim shadows close,
    Life's shadows sombre and sad;
The Guardian Angel, o'er thy couch unseen,
Unfolds his wings — sleep, happy Evaline.

*   *   *   *   *   *

And high among the hills there stood
    A timeworn mansion, dark and grey,
So shrouded in a dusky wood
    That scarce the light of day
Could penetrate its dim and lonely halls,
Or tinge the shrubs that fringed its crumbling walls.

All was so still and solemn here,
  The light wind seemed to hold its breath,
And murmur sadly as in fear;
  The hue and chill of Death
Clung blightingly around each living thing,—
A dreary Winter, without hope of Spring.

A silence over all was thrown,
  That chilled the heart and dimmed the eye,—
The stillness of the churchyard lone
  Without its sanctity;
The groves had grown to forests dense and high,
That veiled from sight the blue and happy sky.

The **light of the All-seeing Eye**
  Smiled not upon the doomèd place,
God's Holy Angels passed it by
  With veiled and shaded face—
The simple peasant shunned its mournful **shade**,
"Ave Maria!" sighed the trembling maid.

A fearful deed within its walls,
    They said, was wrought long years ago;
And still 'mid its decaying halls
    A wailing voice of woe,
At midnight's awful hour, was heard to rise,—
The cry of blood, appealing to the skies!

But dear to its proud owner's heart,
    That solemn, old, ancestral hall;
A thoughtful man, he dwelt apart,
    Unloved, unsought of all;—
Meet lord for those vast forests dusk and grey,
Stately as they, and stateliest in decay.

Lord of that broad and dark domain,—
    Lord of the valley, bright and glad,—
Lord of the mountain and the plain,—
    One only friend he had,
One solitary hope — a little child,
Whose large eyes looked as though they ne'er had
    smiled.

Time was, a fair and lovely face
    Like sunshine stealing 'mid the gloom,
Had shed a soft and tender grace
    About each dismal room :
As flowers with their sweet hues and fragrant breath,
Strewn o'er the bier, lend loveliness to Death.

But o'er her fell the blighting power,
    So meekly fading day by day,
And tranquilly as twilight hour
    She passed from earth away ;
Now in the quaint old church she took her rest,
A weary weight of marble on her breast.

It was a mournful sight to see
    The father and the little lad,
So gloomy, proud, and stately he ;
    The child so mild and sad,
So strong in love, and yet so sorely weak,
So surely fading, yet so sweetly meek.

With what a wordless agony
    That strong man watched this slow decay,
Saw like a phantom gliding by
    His last hope pass away :
Yet shed no tears, though every weary day
His brow grew lined, his black locks gathered grey.

And when the golden sunshine gleamed,
    And softly sighed the summer air,
Clasped to his heart, as though he deemed
    Death could not reach him there,
He'd bear the boy through the long meadow grass,
That he might watch the merry waters pass.

One eve, upon a ruined gate,
    The father and the joyless child
In sorrow and deep silence sate ;—
    The peaceful valley smiled
Through feathery mists that made it yet more sweet,
Tinged with the sunset's glow beneath their feet.

When suddenly an infant's voice,
   As bells of silver, soft and clear,
That seemed to say, "Rejoice, rejoice!"
   Broke lightly on the ear;
And from the waving grass so rich and green,
With beaming face leaped little Evaline.

Her fair and golden head she raised
   In wonder, and a mute surprise;
Awhile the startled children gazed
   Into each other's eyes;
O'er his pale cheek a swift, faint flush was borne,
Like the first glimmer of the early dawn.

Then a quick, sudden cry of joy,—
   It thrilled the father's heart to hear,—
Brake from the wan lips of the boy;—
   An angel's voice drew near,
And 'mid the strains of Nature's Vesper Hymn,
Breathed words of hope and comfort unto him.

" Look up in faith," the sweet voice said,
   " The child thou lovest shall not die ;"
And murmuring through the forest glade,
   The low winds made reply ;
Then all the deep wild prayers he could not speak
Gushed forth in tears upon his pallid cheek.

The day to deepest night succeeds —
   When autumn tinged the forest's shade,
About the daisy-covered meads,
   Two happy children played :
Clasped ever hand in hand the twain were seen,
The feeble Claude and merry Evaline.

PART II.

Long years have rolled away — and still
  In placid beauty smiles the vale,
Still leap the waters down the hill
  Singing their pleasant tale;
In the long grass the fresh and fragrant flowers
Spring forth in shoals, **to** woo the summer showers.

No charm hath faded from the spot,
  The jasmine pale and golden bine,
Yet wave around the lowly cot,—
  Still winds the graceful **vine**
Its fairy tendrils o'er each lattice small,
Scarce through its boughs can peep the whitened **wall**.

A woman fair is Evaline,
    With deep blue, tender, trustful eyes,
Lovely as those with which I ween
    In days of Paradise
The Earth's first Daughter gazed upon her Love,
The while rejoicing angels smiled above.

With dimpled cheek, whose hue is found
    In the rich scented apple-bloom,—
Soft rippling hair, that winding round
    The head can scarce find room,
But longs, as in the Magdalen of old,
To fold her in a robe of billowy gold.

And Claude hath grown to manhood now,
    His tall form hath a languid grace,
Black tresses shade his broad white brow
    And pallid, thoughtful face;
He hath a tongue that can each sense beguile,
Large touching eyes that speak, but never smile.

Seldom he cometh to **the vale,**

 To meet her now — for **all** is changed
From that sweet time, when hill and dale,
 Clasped hand in hand, they ranged,
And wandered o'er — and never — never more
Must he be to her as in days of yore;

She hears them say so — father — all.
 Her hands are folded on her breast,
And o'er her aspect seems to fall
 A something like unrest;
Their cold words have a deadly, blighting power,
Like the first blasts of Winter for the flower.

Her father's **eyes** are waxing dim,
 Grey, scanty locks entwine his brow,
But she, his child, is youth to him,
 Hope — vigour — all things now! —
The day is spent — the golden light is gone,
But still the Star of Eve **shines** brightly on.

 * * * * * *

Amid the dusk hill's sombrous shade
    There lies a wild and rocky glen,
Where nature hath a temple made
    Unsought — untrod of men ;
Huge stony masses loosely piled about,
By mighty trees begirt, shut daylight out.

All day the icy waters drip,
    Slowly from rock to rock they fall,
The dappled deer here cools her lip,
    Nor fears the hunter's call;
Broad waving ferns and moss of richest green,
Lend softened grace unto the solemn scene.

There hangs o'er all a cold grey light,
    No gleam of sunshine gilds the air,
And ever through the silent night
    Black darkness broodeth there ;
Here in her secret haunts, unknown, untrod,—
Sings Nature ever anthems to her God.

Hard by the lonesome glen there lays
    A little, lovely, blest retreat,
You hear the waters dash always—
    Far—far beneath your feet—
In clustered heaps amid their mossy beds
Rich scented violets rear their purple heads.

Broad beeches wave their arms **above,**
    And shed refreshing coolness **there,**
A murmur as of hope and love
    For ever fills the air;
Through the green branches with a softened power,
The sunbeams glisten like an **April** shower.

Here like the spirit of the place,
    When twilight fadeth from the scene,
And starbeams shed a pensive grace,
    Glides gentle Evaline;
Nightly she watches, till the moon on high
In floods of silver bathes the holy sky.

A haunting terror is exprest
   In her blue eye, and changeful cheek,
Her arms are crossed upon her breast,
   Her words are low and meek ;
" Thou of the bleeding heart ! my sorrow see,
Oh Virgin Mother ! bring him back to me !"

All night she prayeth — silently
   God's Angels guard the sleeping Earth,
'Till rise the rose-clouds in the sky
   To hail the morning's birth,—
" Oh Thou of many woes, my sorrow see,
Oh Virgin Mother ! bring him back to me !"

One mournful Evening — sad, alone,
   Came she unto the trysting-place,
And there upon a mossy stone
   (Maria ! grant her grace !)
Among the violets lay a paper white,
Amid their purple heads, it gleamed like light.

Few, formal, were the lines and **cold**—
    (A little will suffice to kill,)
Dense, pall-like mists her frame enfold,
    Death-pangs her bosom thrill,—
In characters of fire these words she read :—
" I have deceived thee, and we are not wed !"

Nor word, nor tear, her feelings told,—
    With dead fixed eye **and lips** apart,
So anguish gathered, 'till it rolled
    Like thunder o'er her heart ;
The reeling **Earth** seemed iron **'neath her tread**,
A brazen sky hung looming overhead.

Then sank she to the ground, and lay
    Like one that is but newly dead,—
Alone, yet not alone—alway
    With azure wings outspread,
The Guardian Angel, weeping, hovered **by,**
And prayed for that poor soul in agony—

She waked to life,— a bitter cry
   Lone Nature, Mighty Mother, heard,
Beneath her bosom, thrillingly,
   A living something stirred;
An icy shudder shivered thro' her frame,
Oh Heaven! she bears a witness of her shame.

How dazzling bright it is! Oh God!
   See how the moonlight streameth down,—
She sees it written on each clod—
   The dusk hills have no frown,
The woods no shade, white brightness fills the air,
No cloud in Heaven—no shadow anywhere.

Then fell a whisper soft and low,—
   An Angel's whisper in her ear,
"Far off the southern breezes blow,
   Come on, and do not fear;
Take up thy cross, be all thy sin forgiven,
This mortal grief shall ope the gates of Heaven."

Her soul was saved — the gushing tears
. Fell fast upon her bosom pale,
With them came thoughts of other years,
    The cottage in the vale ;
" Madonna's blessing be upon thee ever,
But I shall see thee, nevermore — oh, never !"

O'er Heaven there fell a sable pall,
    The moon sank down in sudden shade,
All night about the ruined **Hall**
    The lurid lightning played,
'Till Morn rose gloomily above the scene,
Oh ! whither by its light toiled Evaline ?

PART III.

Still blithely down the vine-clad hills,
    The sparkling waters leap and play,
Their tinkling voice the valley fills
    With melody alway;
The grateful flowers love their joyful song,
And stoop to kiss them, as they glide along.

Jasmine, and woodbine intertwined,
    The snowy cottage walls enfold,
Thro' their long boughs the summer wind
    Sighs gently as of old;
Glad baby-forms around the threshold cling,
And make the welkin with their laughter ring.

There is one other lowly mound,
    Within the churchyard, **calm** and lone,
A poor, forsaken bit of ground,
    That no one cares to own,—
A few neglected flowers around it blow
From a twin **grave—there planted long ago.**

Blow softly, Wintry Winds, above
    That weary, sorrow-stricken breast,
That outlived every human love!
    Mar not his solemn rest;
The peaceful **Evening of his** Day of strife,
For Life to him was Death, and Death was Life.

   *   *   *   *   *

Oh! dear delicious South! how fair
    Thy orange bowers, **thy** olive groves,—
Thy deep blue skies,—thy sunny air!—
    Who loves not thee—naught loves;
The Angels sang for joy when thou wast made,
God's smile is on thee yet—thou canst not fade.

On Baiæ's bright enchanted shore,
    There is a little lonesome grot,
A toppling ruin, white and hoar,
    O'er-canopies the spot;
Ivy and creeping things a wall have made,
That clothes it ever in a dreamy shade.

The deep clear waters of the bay,
    Bluer than Heaven, kiss its base,
The rippling of their waves, alway
    With music fills the place;
Crystals, and dropping seaweeds, passing strange,
Entwine the walls, and o'er the vaulting range.

Around in mournful state arise
    The buried city's hoar remains,
In softened strains the south wind sighs,
    Amid the ruined fanes,
While the dark myrtle, and the flowering bay,
Lend grace to Death, and beauty to Decay.

Here far from kindred — far from **all** —
    (Meet tenant of the peaceful scene),
That could the bitter past recall,
    Dwelt gentle Evaline;
Upon the threshold, rudely carved in wood,
The hallowed sign of the Redemption stood.

Within there rose a little mound,
    A cross upon the mound was laid,
To mark that it was holy ground; —
    What human flower decayed
Amid this tranquil loveliness? **What breast**
From the World's cares had found so sweet a rest?

A Mother's hand that grave had made,
    With stifled cry, and bitter moan,
Uttered in secret, and in shade,
    Marked but by God alone;
In the dense masses of her golden hair,
Her infant limbs she wrapped — then laid him there.

And with him every joy, and strife,
    And hope, that bound her to the sod,
She buried too, then vowed her life
    As consecrate to God;
The tears of blood that bathed her nameless Dead,
Were the last drops her eyes on Earth might shed.

Then forth in confidence and faith,
    With cross in hand she went — where'er
The cry arose of woe, and death,
    Of misery, and care —
'Mid fever gaunt, and madness' fiercer thrall,
Naught could her spirit quell — her heart appal.

As balmy winds that healing leave,
    As summer rains to parching dell,
As dropping dews of kindly Eve,
    Her gentle presence fell;
Men called her "Angel" — saw around her head,
The light of other worlds already shed.

Were there no times, the bitter Past
   Rose like a phantom to her gaze,—
A basilisk, to scare and blast
   The quiet of her days?
When haunting memories, fatal to her peace,
Cried with a wailing voice that would not cease?

"Oh, blessèd days and dreams **of yore**!
   Oh, golden years of love and truth!
Oh, Father, country, mine no more!
   Oh, husband of my youth!
Oh, vain, vain longing for the rest that none
On earth may know—the Dead have rest alone!"

Such times there were—but brief their stay,
   The wounded spirit cried "How long?"
And seraph voices seemed to say,
   "Poor struggling soul, be strong,
The night is waning fast—the Dawn is **nigh,**
Far off we see the rose-clouds in the sky."

PART IV.

One tranquil Autumn Eve—the sun
    Had sunk in clouds of amber hue,
And still his golden glories shone
    'Mid Heaven's deepening blue;
Star after star stole forth its guard to keep,
Like Angels' eyes that watch o'er Nature's sleep.

A dreamy calm was in the air,
    The wind's light murmur was not heard,
The vine and olive moveless were,
    The waters were not stirred;
The clouds were motionless, and the broad bay,
A sea of rainbow hues, unruffled lay.

The peaceful beauty of the hour
    Sank on the soul of Evaline,
With soft'ning and consoling power;
    Rose many a bygone scene
To memory's vision, of the Home that lay
Beyond the shadowy mountains, far away.

Dear forms that Death had long laid low
    Seemed floating round—a loving band,
Clad in the raiments white as snow
    Of the far Spirit-land;
To her rapt view, each golden cloud that streamed
O'er the blue sky, was fraught with the Redeemed.

O'er Nature's dark'ning face—o'er Heaven,
    She saw the Armies of the Blest,
The countless Hosts of the Forgiven,
    Ascending to their rest;
'Till lost at length, in shades of gathering night,
A shower of silv'ry stars brake on her sight.

Then to the shadow of her cave,
    She meekly turned, to kneel and pray;
Upon the little flower-strewn grave
    The glancing moonlight lay;
Softly she murmured—" Never unto me
May'st thou return, but I shall go to thee."

The cold grey shadows gathered round,
    A light breeze kissed the placid Deep,
That with a sad and mournful sound
    Waked from its charmèd sleep;
The last faint rose-hue faded from the sky,
And all was dark, save the All-seeing Eye.

She slept, if slumber could be deemed
    That fixed suspension of the breath,
More like some spell-bound trance it seemed,
    Or temporary death!
What solemn visions, mystical and dread,
Scared peace from sleep, and quiet from her bed?

She saw the pallid moonshine grow
 More dazzling—exquisitely bright,
'Till Earth and Heaven, in one glow
 Of white and blinding light,
Were flooded o'er—her wrapt eye seemed to scan
Beyond the stars, that glimmered pale and wan.

And voices, like the rushing Wind,
 And many thunders deep and strong,
The whirlwind, and the storm combined,
 Pealed all the Spheres among
In awful concert joined—with one accord,
" Holy, and Just, and True, how long, O Lord?"

They ceased — and rose before her sight,
 A mountain-range—some grey and hoar,
With ice, and wasteless snow, were white;
 And some, all mantled o'er
With olive forests, and the dropping bine,
Breathed but of Human trust and love Divine.

One darker, mightier than the rest,
    Plunged in the skies its cloven brow,
A lurid flame enwreathed its crest
    And tinged the clouds below;
While seething fire-tracks, desolate and wild,
Twined its scorched heights whereon no verdure smiled.

Mile upon mile, till far away
    In space and Ocean lost, there rolled
The billows of a mighty bay,
    All robed in moonlight cold,—
And on its shores, a crescent city showed
All white and glittering, as a silv'ry cloud.

Street upon street, tower upon tower,
    And palace proud, and stately spire,
And statued court, and trellised bower,
    Glowed in that pallid fire,
That glory beam,— she heard the fountains play,
And saw ascending high, their starry spray.

But as she gazed, o'er Heaven there fell
    A sudden shadow, and the sea
Heaved with a deep, and troubled swell;
    Pale phantoms seemed to flee
Thro' the dense air, while girded with the storm,
And robed in **Darkness,** rose an Awful Form.

Fierce lightnings round his pathway played,
    And fiery pillars 'neath him bent;
A gleaming rainbow crowned his head,
    And spanned **the Firmament;**
Before the glories of his brow divine,
The stars grew dark, the moonbeams ceased **to shine.**

He passed—the Angel of the Lord,
    A moment o'er the City bowed,
Then smote it with a flaming sword:
    A cry so long, so loud,
Ne'er rose before to the Eternal Throne,
(A thousand death-shrieks gathered into one.)

As that, that roused her from her trance;—
    She waked—what sounds were in her ear?
The rippling water's gentle dance,
    The soft wind's soughing near,
And low, sweet voices that went murmuring by,
" The rose-clouds gather fast, the Morn is nigh."

PART V.

The morning mists rolled **cold and white**,
   In phantom shapes o'er vale **and lea**,—
A lonely Woman on a height
   Washed by the hollow sea,—
Far 'neath her feet a crescent city showed
In the pale twilight, like a spectral cloud.

And 'neath the wan stars' fading beams
   The blasted mountain reared its head,
Its dark sides wreathed with fiery streams,
   And vapours lurid red
While morning brightened on the valleys **low**,
Black night hung looming on its awful brow.

There were the mountains hoar and grey,
    The green and village-dotted vales,
The rolling waters of the Bay
    Alive with snowy sails,—
The vine-clad hills — the silv'ry olive woods,
The church-crowned heights, and convent solitudes.

A dreamy stillness brooded round,
    No hum, no voice, the city gave,
No murmur, save one mournful sound,
    The beating of the wave;
What thoughts were her's,—lone wanderer on the height,
What scenes prophetic swam before her sight?

How yearned her spirit for its rest,
    Its promised rest of peace and love!
As yearned above the watery waste
    Unto the Ark the dove;
Or, as one dying upon arid plains,
That dreams of dropping dews and balmy rains.

Not earthward must **she turn or shrink,**
   Yet mingled not in her deep prayer;
The cavern on the Ocean's brink,
   The Angel watching there,
Whose large fair wings a crystal glimmer shed,
About the pillow of the Infant Dead?

She meekly clasped the Cross she **bore**—
   There stole a whisper o'er the sea;
"Come **on,** upon the Spirit-Shore
   Thy Sisters wait for thee!"
Come on! Divinely Led! before thee gleams
The Promised Land, the City of thy dreams.

The morning mists **have passed and fled,**
   The sun pours down a blinding heat,—
Is it a City of the Dead?
   No busy tramp of feet,
No voice, no sound of teeming life to tell,
But the deep booming of one solemn bell.

The Sun shines on, a blinding red,
    And round the Church-doors opened wide,
In groups, the Dying and the Dead
    Lie huddled side by side ;
The air is thick with parting souls—their cry
Goes ever, ever, upward to the sky.

The palace gates stand open,—there
    The beggar hides his sinking head ;
Its halls are tenantless, though fair,
    The owners all have fled ;
" Fly ! fly ! " How fast the curse speeds on behind—
No time to think of mercy — kindred — kind.

The sun drops down in clouds of flame,
    Around the brooding shadows swim ;
But night and day are all the same,
    Night brings no rest to Him,—
The Dread Destroyer, on his unseen way,
Night brings no hope,— would God that it were day !

The priest grows weary at his prayer—
 Dies on the ear the ghostly hymn—
More faint the funeral torches glare,
 'Till all is dark, and dim,
And hushed—save that one thrilling, bitter moan,
The low death-wail, that ever crieth on.

Who moves amid the ghastly scene,
 Amid the storm a blessèd calm?
Whose low, soft words and looks serene
 Fall on the soul like balm?
Who shrinks not from the foul and tainted breath—
The lazar-touch—the loathsomeness of Death?

Go on,—thou meek and quiet One,
 Each death-drop that thou wipest now,
Shall shine as God's resplendent **Sun**
 Hereafter round thy brow!
Each parting blessing breathed by dying men,
Shall be an Angel's song to greet thee then.

  * * * * *

A chamber in a palace-home,—
    A nuptial chamber gay and bright,
With richest webs of rarest loom,
    And costly Art bedight;
Softly the silvery moonbeams glance and play
O'er flashing gems,— and flowers,— and rich array.

A stately chamber, as beseems
    A noble Bride, so pure and fair:
The Sun with his own glory beams
    Hath dyed her golden hair,
And the deep azure of the Autumn skies
Dwells in the tender depths of her sweet eyes.

She lies upon her Bridegroom's breast,
    One round, white arm around him thrown,
The other in his clasp is pressed;
    But, oh! no voice — no tone
To tell of love — the Blessing, and the Blest!
Look on her pale blue lips — why speak the rest?

And he—he, too, is dying fast,
    Forsaken in his palace-home;
His mind hath wandered to the Past;
    What mocking visions come?
What scenes forgotten—faded Memories—
The ghosts of buried years around him rise!

How fast the phantoms come and go,
    And press upon his fevered brain!
What long-hushed voices, faint and low,
    Fall on his ear again?
There by his side his stately Father stands,
With mournful, loving eyes, and folded hands.

He wanders 'mid his native hills,
    With her,—his first, his early Love;
He hears the music of the rills,
    The soft wind's sigh above;
Her long rich curls are streaming o'er his arm,
Rain on his cheek her kisses soft and warm.

A white-thatched cottage in a vale,
    An old man watching at the door,
From dewy morn 'till Even pale,
    For her who comes no more ;
Oh, Man ! remorseless ! — Spirit unforgiven !
That patient look shall drive thee back from Heaven.

A rushing river, deep and strong,
    Whose waves are foul and black as sin,
Above — around, they heave and throng,
    And all his breath draw in ;
And ever 'mid the roar and tumult wild,
A prayerful voice — a woman's — Angel mild.

What stands between him and the Night ?
    'Tis Evaline — his early love !
Around her shines a glory light, —
    The light of worlds above ;
It is no dream — her kisses, soft and meek
As summer showers, are raining on his cheek.

"Oh! shall our Blessèd God forgive
    E'en those who hung His Son on tree;
And shall I nought to thee forgive,
    Who art a part of me?
Ah, me! how fast the Life within him dies!
Oh! Claude, belovèd! bless me with thine eyes!"

She wipes the death-dews from his face,
    That gather there so strong and fast;
Their lips meet in one long embrace,
    The purest, and the last;
A sudden shadow veils the moonlit room,
What Awful Presence moves amid the gloom?

Nought sees she clear of shape or form,
    A something undefined and vast,
A blackness like the brooding Storm
    In Autumn skies o'ercast—
And on her shrinking breast a hand of bone,
An icy touch,—that chills her heart to stone.

"Glory to Heaven," her wan lips say,
   "Glory to Heaven," the rose-clouds dawn,
They crimson all the twilight grey,
   And brighten into morn;
Deeper, and deeper yet,—till all the skies
Glow in the purple light of Paradise.

And see—in raiments white as snow,
   And brows star-wreathed—a loving band,—
They call her with their voices low
   Unto the Angel Land;
Their voices low and tender: "Sister, dear,
The dreary night is past,—the Morn is here.

"Rest, weary Soul! for never more
   'Mid storm and strife thy path shall be;
Calm dwells upon the Spirit Shore—
   'There shall be no more sea!'
No cloud shall dim thy skies,—no tempest frown,
Thy sun shall no more set—thy Moon go down."

MADELON.

PART I.

A SPRING-TIDE morn with beauty rife,—
   The gorgeous sun a halo threw
O'er all that waked to light and life,
   And robed them in a hue
Of warmth and golden glory, till they shone
With a bright tenfold gladness scarce their own.

A time when sweet and holy **thought**
    Within the chastened soul hath birth,
Breathing of peace and calmness — fraught
    With more of Heaven than Earth;
When this fair world and the bright skies above,
Proclaim aloud to man **his Maker's** love.

All things the shape of gladness **took** —
    Music was in the wind's low sigh,
In the quick rushing of the **brook,**
    That danced right merrily;
And rustling leaves sent forth a pleasant sound,
And all was melody — above — around.

Sweet sounds more eloquent than words,
    Rang out from groves and waving woods;
A song of joy from countless birds,
    In their green solitudes;
And children's laughter on the soft breeze borne,
From glowing fields rich with the rising corn.

And fair wild-flowers of every hue
    Put forth new beauties to the sight,
Yet drooped and laden with the dew
    Of the past starry night;
And some to which that night had given birth,
Looked forth for the first time upon the earth.

A Bridal morn! the marriage-bell
    Sends forth its blithe and pleasant tone —
Wake, Echo, wake! in mossy dell
    The woodland still and lone;
Wake, Echo, wake! thy mystic voices round,
'Till the warm-scented air is rife with sound.

The whispering youth,— the blushing maid,
    The fair child with his face of glee,
The hoary-haired,— the matron staid,
    Are here to welcome thee;
Then forth, young Bride, weep not thy home to leave,
His love shall shelter thee — why dost thou grieve?

No darkening cloud hangs o'er thee now,
    Bright sunlight glitters o'er thy path ;
The Bridal wreath is on thy brow,—
    Tones such as Love's voice hath
Fall on thine ear—fond arms around thee fold—
What thoughts are in thy breast ? what fears untold ?

Think'st thou of voices that no more
    Shall greet thee in thy stranger-home ?
Of dear, kind **voices, that of yore**
    Were ever wont to come
In pleasant muster round thy household hearth,
To soothe thy every grief, and share thy mirth ?

Think'st thou of her, **whose fair,** mild brow
    Hung o'er thee in thy childhood's days,
Who taught thee first thy knee to bow
    In holy prayer and praise ?
Weep'st thou she is not here her child to bless,
And share with thee thy tearful happiness ?

Droop not! sure none could gaze on thee—
    Thy fair, slight form—thy bridal guise—
Thy gentle smile so sweet to see —
    Thy deep blue pleading eyes—
Thy timid look of trusting tenderness,—
And feel not thou wast formed to love—to bless.

There is a murmur, soft and low,
    Of broken voices, sweet—yet sad,
"Heaven's blessing, maiden, with thee go,"
    They weep, who'd fain be glad,
'Tis o'er—take her, young Lover for thine own,
Sound blithely, Bells.—Alas! poor Madelon!

PART II.

It was a calm, still Autumn eve,
    The red sun 'mid his clouds of gold
Yet lingered, as though loth to leave
    That village lone and old,
Though light, fantastic mists were stealing on,
And the pale stars were rising one by one.

His touch yet lingered on the trees,
    That waved their shadowy arms aloft,
And answered to the wanton breeze
    In murmurs low and soft;
A crimson glow unto the streamlet gave,
And bathed in golden hues each tiny wave.

Sweet sounds were wafted from afar,—
    The child's light laugh — the village hum,
Yet scarcely could the stillness mar,
    So faintly did they come;
Blent with the tinkling of the sheepfold's bell,
Borne on the gale from many a mossy dell.

The old church wore a pleasant look
    As o'er it the last sunbeams brake,
With cheerful caw the glossy rook,
    A parting glance to take,
Perched on its ivied tower, so worn and gray,
Ere to his far-off nest he winged his way.

No well-carved stone here reared its head —
    The cypress, like a funeral-pall,
Waved its dark boughs above the dead,
    And they were nameless all;
Nor needed they the aid of sculptured art,
Whose names were graved in many a human heart.

MADELON.

The clear, pale moon is throned on high,
　　The birds unto their nests have flown —
　The cool night-winds sweep freshly by —
　　Yet lingers Madelon ;
Nought breaks the stillness that now reigns around,
Save her light footfall on the dewy ground.

A sound ! was it his footstep ? **No !**
　　'Twas but the echo of her own,
　She to her weary couch must go
　　Deserted and alone ;
Yet he had met her once, and old thoughts o'er
His cold heart rushing — clasped her as of yore.

　But few brief months had sped and flown,
　　Since fondly — proudly by his side,
　His loved — his beautiful — his own —
　　He'd led her forth **a Bride !**
But heaviness untold, and secret tears,
Had wrought upon her brow the work of years.

Alas! the deep and heavy grief
    That slowly wears the heart away,
To which the night brings no relief,
    That shuns the light of day,
And masks itself in smiles, like flowers that wave
Above the gloom and darkness of the grave.

To lade a bark with all we love,
    And launch it forth 'neath sunny skies,
Then see the clouds grow dark above,
    And the black tempest rise,
The scathing lightnings leap — wave after wave
Dash o'er, and we all-impotent to save.

To hear the voice most dearly prized,
    Most cherished, — most beloved of all —
Watched, listened for — on all beside
    In gentle accents fall
As once it did for us, in times of old,
Frame for our ear alone harsh words and cold.

To see the stern and loveless eye—
    Watch day by day our hopes decay,
All we have deemed reality
    Pass like a dream away,—
To find the light we've followed from afar,
A meteor false—our sun a falling star.

To see our hopes in ruin laid —
    The sunlight of existence gone;—
To feel that we have been betrayed,
    And **still—and still love on,**
Hoping all—daring all, for its dear sake,
Oh! these are things that crush the heart—not break!

All these were hers—yet still she strove
    To veil from all her wretchedness,
With smiles of fond and anxious love
    Her aching brow to dress;
Nor ever murmur from her sweet lips brake,
But low and pleasant were the words she spake.

Alas, young Bride! thy cheek's rich bloom
　　Must fade,—thy fair head droop in vain;—
Thy sun of hope hath set in gloom,
　　It ne'er may rise again;
Smile on with thy soft smile so sweet and sad,
It smites upon the heart thou seek'st to glad.

Hope on for what may never be!
　　The love that thou shalt know no more,
No gentle arm shall circle thee
　　As once it did of yore;
No loving breast shall form thy pillow now,
No warm and glowing kiss light on thy brow.

Heed not the jest, the sarcasm rude,
　　Go, strain thine infant to thy breast,
Lone partner of the solitude
　　That he hath rendered blest,
For in thy bitterest moments thou hast smiled
With joy to clasp the Father in the child.

His soft cheek on thy bosom prest,
　　Dream thou of joys that ne'er may be,
Of days of sweet and blessèd rest
　　That thou may'st never see.—
Morn in her golden veil is stealing on,
He comes not yet.—Alas, poor Madelon!

PART III.

Night, lovely Night! her veil had thrown
    O'er the still earth,—the heavens on high,
The stars stole forth all one by one
    Gemming the quiet sky;
Their pale rays shadowed in the stream, that bound
By mossy banks, sent forth a silvery sound.

All things were robed in moonlight pale—
    The star-crowned hills—the dark green woods—
The nodding grove—the quiet vale—
    And forest solitudes—
The fading flower, and that of one hour's birth,
That drank for the first time the dews of earth.

And sweet, low sounds alone were heard,
    The light wind floated gently by—
The dark leaves by its soft breath **stirred,**
    Made pleasant melody,
And shook the gathering dew from spray to spray,
That flashed like gems beneath the moon's chaste ray.

Night, tranquil Night! when solemn **thought**
    And feelings high to man are given,
Breathing **of happier** worlds,—and fraught
    With less **of Earth** than Heaven;
When Nature tired in calm and stillness lies,
A holy hour—the Sabbath of the skies!

Night, solemn Night! when those long wept,—
    The loved—the mourned—the missed of yore,
Wake from the sleep they long have slept,
    To visit us once more;
And lips that long have mouldered **'neath the clay,**
Cling to our **own** as though they'd cling for **aye.**

Within a chamber dark and lone,
    There sits a form so worn and wan,
The grave might claim it for its own —
    God bless thee, Madelon!
An unseen form is hovering round thee now,
His darkening shadow falls upon thy brow!

The worm lies darkly 'neath the bloom
    That dyes her thin and hollow cheek,
Consumption pale — decay — and doom
    Lurk in its hectic streak;
The light of other worlds is o'er her shed,
Yet of the Living — numbered with the Dead.

Thoughts that the dying only know
    Are hers — a sad and solemn band —
And gentle voices soft and low,
    From the far Spirit-land,
Around her float; sweet tones to memory dear,
Long hushed and mute, are stealing on her ear.

Dear faces long forgotten — how
    With Angel-smiles, they round her glide, —
Gigantic shadows o'er her bow —
    Strange forms are at her side; —
Vast and unearthly shapes, and phantoms dread,
Stalk by her shrinking frame with noiseless tread.

None nigh to dry the starting tear, —
    With kind caress or gentle word,
To soothe and calm her spirit's fear —
    And he — her bosom's lord;
Alas! her head is bowed, — her eye is dim
With weary watching, the long night for him.

Where lingers he? amid the crowd —
    To hope, to sense, to feeling lost,
Where lust, and vice, and revel loud,
    With their foul, baneful host,
Inflict on human hearts that throb and live
A darker curse than deepest hell can give.

The moon is down — the gorgeous sun
   Bursts through the twilight grey and dim,
In glittering pomp his course to run;
   On high the matin hymn
Ascends from far, — a sweet and joyous strain,
Nature rejoicing, — morn is come again!

But hark! a dull and heavy sound —
   The muffled tread of many feet
Breaketh the holy calm around:
   Wildly her pulses beat!
She lists! her thin and bloodless lips apart,
The worm already busy at her heart.

They pause, and cross the threshold now,
   She cannot stir, but trembling stands,
Her aching head and throbbing brow
   Clasped by her icy hands;
She sees the still and shrouded form they bear,
Nor question asks, — she feels that Death is there.

Gone to his long and silent rest—
    To the unknown bourne lone and dim,
  Far from the fond and loving breast
    That ached to pillow him;
'Mid riot wild, from sin and guilt unshriven,
To meet his God—unblest and unforgiven.

  The cold, calm loveliness of Death—
    Its awful, statue-like repose;—
  The smile unbroken by a breath,
    Whose very beauty throws
A chill on living hearts, she sees—one cry
Bursts from her lips of bitter agony.

  The sole,—most cherished **link is riven,**
    The last that bound her **to the sod—**
  Rest for the weary is in Heaven,
    Then, Spirit, to thy God!
Her thin white fingers wander o'er his brow,
His breast her pillow,—all is silence now.

    *   *   *   *   *

There is a spot so quaint and lone,
    So quiet in its loveliness,
So shady, calm, and moss-o'ergrown,—
    So formed to soothe and bless;
'Twould seem that from the realms of guilt and fear
Sweet Peace had flown and found a haven here.

Here strife and clamour never come,
    But soft, low sounds alone were heard;
The faint and far-off village hum,
    The carol of the bird,
The leafy music of the ancient trees,
The tinkling brook, the murmur of the breeze.

One lowly mound—one lonely grave
    Is there in golden verdure drest,
The fairest flowers around it wave,
    As though they loved it best;
As if the loveliest blossoms did arise
From gentlest hearts, and holiest sympathies.

The setting sun around it throws
    His last faint beams of golden light,
And o'er its calm and deep repose
    The stars keep watch by night;
Life's toil is o'er — her weary task is done,
And she sleeps well.—Alas, poor Madelon!

MISCELLANEOUS POEMS.

LEGEND OF THE UNTERSBERG.

There are many romantic traditions and legends attached to the mountains in the neighbourhood of Saltzburg. One of the most beautiful is that of the Untersberg, in whose mysterious caverns, according to popular belief Charlemagne (Karl der Grosse) and the Emperor Charles V. repose in a magic sleep, from which they will awaken and come forth, when Germany, restored to her pristine fame and glory, shall again form a United Empire.

I STOOD upon the Untersberg, one dreamy summer even,
The sun was sinking down in the hazy, purple heaven;
A calm was in the air, like the peace of souls forgiven.

And dimly in the distance the hoary peaks arose,
The mighty Alpine chain, white with everlasting snows,
Whose wild, untrodden haunts, God their Maker only knows.

There hung a soft and tender haze of ever-changing hue,
Sweet rose-tints blending strangely with faint unearthly blue
O'er all the lower hills, where the piny forests grew.

And far beneath my feet, touched with pale and pearly light,
Uprose the rocky Mönchsberg, its castle-crowned height
And sister-summit, capped o'er with convents hoar and white.

And nestled in between them the ancient city * lay,
A crimson sunbeam tinted its church-spires tall and grey,
And streaked the rapid river—rushing wildly on its way.

O'er swelling fields of waving corn, and meadows rich with hay,
O'er countless gardens dotted o'er with châlets white and gay,
That filled the smiling valleys, shone the dying light of day.

The lowing herds of cattle, their homeward-pathway trod,
The fireflies spangled o'er the flower-enamelled sod,
The soughing winds and streams sang their Vesper Hymns to God.

* Saltzburg.

The peasant sate before his door, to pass the hour of rest,
And kissed the laughing faces that nestled to his breast,
And humbly as he did so, the Gracious Giver blest.

But as I gazed upon them—a sweet and charmèd breeze
Came sighing perfume-laden—thro' the lofty forest trees,
That all my spirit lapped in a soft and dreamful ease.

The landscape faded slowly, in cold grey shadows thrown,
I saw the mighty peak open wide its hoary crown,
And sank within its depths—down, a thousand fathoms down;

Down sinking, ever sinking, in silence and alone,
Thro' darkness ever deep'ning, 'till to pitchy blackness grown—
I heard the rushing torrents in their hollow caverns moan;

Down sinking, ever sinking, I heard the waters knock,
And wildly beating ever, their prison-house of rock,
Whose granite walls re-echoed the fury of the shock.

But ever thro' the darkness—I saw the pallid gleam
Of stars in depths of ether—and every shining beam
As Angels' watchful eyes—to my failing sense did seem.

Then all the vision changing—I stood within a cave
Whose vault of hanging crystals a fitful lustre gave,
As moonshine glimmering o'er the rippling of the wave.

And spiry columns tall, of an ever-changing sheen,
Bright sapphire, gleaming onyx, and glowing emerald green—
In endless shapes of beauty round the magic Hall were seen.

And still beneath me fiercely, I heard the torrents roar,
And saw the beryl waves—thro' the white transparent floor
Of purest alabaster—wrought mystically o'er.

And side by side two masses—white as never-melting snows,
Of smooth and polished rock, wreathed with purple flame arose,
Where lay two crownèd shapes—locked in deep and still repose.

With closed unmoving eyelid—with fixed, suspended breath,
With folded hands unstirred by the massive chest beneath,
And calm unchanging smile—all Death's stillness without Death.

I knew those princely brows whereon Truth and Justice reign,
I knew those stately traits that all loyal hearts retain,
I knew the Fifth Great Karl—Imperial Charlemagne.

The Vision slowly faded in shadows cold and grey,
And Spirit-voices sweetly to my spirit seemed to say,
" Yet dimly thro' the night, gleams the promise of the day."

JOSEPHINE AT THE FOUNTAIN.

In a remote village of Switzerland, there exists a fountain whose waters gush forth at uncertain intervals. It is called by the peasants the " Wishing Fountain." The legend runs, that if the fountain plays immediately after a wish has been formed, the request will be granted. It is reported that the Empress Josephine spent a whole night by **the side of this fountain in the vain hope of seeing its waters play**.

  T<small>HE</small> Sun yet lingering in the West,
   In gold hath robed the sky,
  Light clouds in hues of purple drest
   Are sailing slowly by,—
  Stars, o'er the dark hill's grassy crest
   Are rising silently—

JOSEPHINE AT THE FOUNTAIN.

O'er darksome glen, o'er waving wood,
   The mild moon palely glows —
O'er the dim forest's solitude
   Night's sable shadows close;
Scarce doth a sound of Life intrude
   To mar the deep repose.

The lowing of the far-off herd,
   The clear brook rushing by —
The sweet note of some hidden bird,
   The light wind's gentle sigh —
'Mid trees and flowers that faintly stirred
   Scarce murmur in reply.

The rippling of some hidden stream,
   The river deep and clear —
Tones, like the murmurs in a dream
   From the dim forests near,
Sounds that make stillness deeper seem,
   Alone fall on the ear.

JOSEPHINE AT THE FOUNTAIN.

The peasant's day of toil is **o'er,**
  He to his rest hath gone,
Yet by that rock, so dark and hoar,
  Lingers that lonely one,
With pale, sad features, **that no more**
  The glad smile brightens on.

Her white hands o'er her bosom laying
  As the big tears **start,**
Ever—ever—ever praying
  Heaven might change his heart,
Heavy words her pale lips saying—
  "**Oh** God!—'tis hard **to part."**

And still beside that pebbly bed,
  It is her bitter lot,
To watch with bowed and weary **head**
  For that which cometh not;—
No stream—save those her eyes **may shed,**
  Hot—burning on the spot.

JOSEPHINE AT THE FOUNTAIN.

The twilight shades have fleeted now,
 The flowers with dew **are wet,**
Each dark hill wears upon its brow
 A **starry coronet ;**
But still the weary knees must bow —
 The waters come not **yet.**

Here oft the shy maid's footsteps fall,
 Glad voices gaily **ring,**
For ever — ever — at their call,
 Doth flow the blessèd spring ;
She — she alone — the *One* of all —
 Watcheth vainly — sorrowing.

Morn's soft winds are freshly playing,
 Slowly Night's dim shades depart —
Her white brow on the cold rock laying,
 Still, the bitter tear-drops **start** ;
Ever watching — ever praying,
 Heaven might change his heart.

MURMURING.

Eve, peaceful Eve! the red and gorgeous sun
   Hath set in beauty in the curtained West,
His course of blessing and of glory run,
   All Nature sinks to calm, and holy rest;
The pale moon mounts her studded throne on **high,**
And bathes in silv'ry tints the quiet sky.

Sweet things are here—the dark and leafy woods,
   By elfin bright or fay-feet trod alone,
The stately forests' ancient solitudes,
   With all their store of birds and flowers unknown,—
Green shady haunts—the fountain lone and old,
Where many a tale of passion has been told.

Sweet sounds are here—the waving of the trees—
   Voices in bank and hedge from unseen things—
The gentle whisper of the passing breeze—
   The light and scarce-heard rush of insect wings—
The rushing brook — the clear and babbling spring,
Oft hid from sight, but ever murmuring.

A young girl gazed upon the silent night,
   On the hushed beauty of the star-lit sky,
Voiceless and moveless —with the wan moonlight
   Reflected in her deep and proud blue eye;
Her head was bent and bowed — her lip comprest —
Her thin white hands were clasped upon her breast;

Her cheek was flushed and hot, decay was there,
   Lurking all deadly 'neath its vivid bloom;
Her brow was arched, and high, and dazzling fair,
   But o'er it fell the shadow of the tomb:
With the mind's eye, ye might have traced thereon
The skeleton outline of a hand of bone.

She spake at last,—"Oh it is hard to die,
    When all things round of hope and beauty speak,
Spring-tide is come,—I feel—I know 'tis nigh;
    Its fresh warm breath falls softly on my cheek:
I hear its harbingers breathe forth their vows,
In the deep shadows of the waving boughs.

"All things of gladness tell—the stars **above**
    Look down in paly splendour and rejoice,
The lone green woods send forth a song of **love,**
    The dark and rushing streams lift up their **voice;**
O'er earth—o'er sky there breathes the same sweet strain,
Nature rejoicing, 'Spring hath come again.'"

"Oh! it is hard to die so young, so loved!
    In the dark land of silence to sink down,
From love—from joy—from hope alike removed,
    Where all things are forgotten and unknown,
The dank cold earth my pillow and my bed,
No kindred, save the pale and mouldering Dead.

MURMURING.

"Is it thy hand, dear Mother, that is prest
   So gently, on my cold and aching brow?
Oh, let me — let me lean upon thy breast,
   Strange shapes and forms are floating round me now,
Dim shadows — gliding in the moon's pale ray,
And spectral hands, that beckon me away.

"And Thou, best loved — I feel thy hand in mine,
   Thy gentle voice falls sweetly on mine ear;
I feel thy loving arms around me twine,
   Thy lips kiss from my cheek the falling tear,
Low words thou breathest — telling unto me
How blest we once have been — and yet might be.

"Oh, cherished hopes of Youth — oh, dear day-dreams,
   Sweet days of yore — come back to me again?
Ah! worse than vain — no star of hope there beams
   Through the deep shadows of this night of pain!"
Hush! solemn voices whisper in reply —
"Seek peace in Heaven." — Oh God, I cannot die!

RESIGNATION.

Eve, tranquil Eve! the red and gorgeous sun
   Yet lingered in the deep empurpled West,
While thro' the gathering twilight grey and dun,
   Rose slowly o'er the dark hills' grassy crest
The pale and solemn stars.—The soft wind swept
The cheek like balm—Nature one Sabbath kept.

Eve, starry, tranquil Eve! the hour of hours
   For sweet and holy thoughts of peace and love,
When for a space is lent this world of our's
   The dreamy beauty of the worlds above;
A holy presence seemeth nigh—all Earth
Looks calm and pure as at Creation's birth.

The timid birds had breathed their last sweet vows,
　　And scarce a sound brake on the listening ear,
Save the light rustling of the laden boughs,
　　The silvery voices of the streamlet clear,
Or breeze-borne echoes of the sheepfold's bell,
Wafted from far, o'er many a flower-strewn dell.

Stole slowly forth the citizens of night,—
　　Its dizzy rounds the dark-winged beetle flew,
The starry glowworm reared its glittering light,
　　The white-winged moths their airy circles drew,
The tiny field-mouse left its mossy nook,
The drowsy bat its gloomful haunt forsook.

A Spirit-voice seemed breathing all around—
　　From the still lake, lit by the moon's pale beams,
From vale and dell stole forth that silvery sound,
　　Blent with the music of the woods and streams;
The holy hymn uprising from the sod,
Of loving Nature to a loving God.—

RESIGNATION.

A still and silent room — how hushed — how **cold** !
   It is not dark — and yet on all around
A nameless shadow falls — here youth grown old,
   Like seed untimely blighted in the ground —
Or blossom lightning rent, lies withering,
Night while 'tis **day — and** Winter while 'tis Spring.

With wan and heavy brow, and hollow cheek,
   Pain-racked and tortured — yet so sweetly mild —
Bowed and worn down — life-weary — yet as meek,
   Docile, and gentle as a little child ;
With not one care for Earth, or the Earth's strife,
Save but to them, to whom her Life *is* Life.

All dank, and heavy droops **the clustering hair,**
   O'er the pale cheek, the white and clammy **brow,**
The slimy earth-worm soon shall revel there,
   Death's dark'ning hues are gath'ring o'er them now ;
The shadow of the Tomb **is o'er her** shed,
On Earth, not of Earth — Sister of the Dead.

Her head rests heavily upon *his* breast,
   Its best-loved pillow : on his marble cheek,
In his strained eyes, no scalding tear-drops rest,
   But thoughts are in his heart tongue ne'er may speak :
Calm — cold — and rigid as the icebound lake,
His is the grief that crusheth — doth not break.

She moves — she stirs — her white arms round him fold,
   As she would cling for aye, and never part.
What thoughts — what hopes — what dread — what fears untold —
   Unguessed — unknown — are throbbing at her heart!
Before her eyes, what nameless terrors glide, —
What gaunt and spectral form is at her side !

The air is thick with Death — pale faces gleam
   Around on every side — the Lost — the Dead —
All wan and earthy in the cold moonbeam,
   Glide round her ever with a noiseless tread ; —
Loved forms that long have mouldered 'neath the clay,
In shroud and gravecloth, beckon her away.

Sweet seraph voices ever soft and low,
   Like echoes of the melody **of Heaven,**
Strains that the Dead to Earth alone may **know,**
   Breathing of hope — of rest — of sins forgiven,
And memory-haunting tones — the lost — the dear,
Blent with **those** strains, are stealing on her ear.

She speaks at last : — " **The stars are in the skies,**
   That never — nevermore shall rise **for me,**
Nor moon, nor stars, nor blessèd sweet sunrise,
   These worn and weary eyes again may see ;
So few my sands of life, a child might tell
Their numbers o'er — Earth, take my last farewell.

" And Thou, belovèd — clasp **me once again,**
   More closely yet unto thy loving **breast ;** —
Dying in youth — all feeling merged in pain !
   But in *thy* arms, I yet **am very blest ;**
Thro' every vein there creeps Death's **icy chill** —
I see thee not — oh, let me *feel* thee still.

RESIGNATION.

"Weep not, dear Mother, bless me ere I die,
 I feel thy burning hands in mine are prest —
I go where never tear may dim the eye —
 Where sorrow comes not — where the weary rest;
Thy scalding tears fall fast upon my brow —
One kiss — another — all is Darkness now."

THE VILLAGE SABBATH.

A **HOLY** morn—the Sabbath bell
    Sends forth its clear and pleasant tone,
Far o'er the green and **mossy** dell,
    The woodland still and lone;
Breathing of holiness—of peace and love,
Of hope upon the earth—of joy above.

The air is full of melody,
    The waving woods **are** rife **with song,**
The light wind floateth merrily
    The dark green boughs among;
And cheerily the clear, half-hidden brook,
Winds its swift way through many a mossy nook.

THE VILLAGE SABBATH.

The village stream is robed in gold,
    The sunbeams o'er its surface glance,
And lovely things their hues unfold,
    And o'er its waters dance;
Sweeping its sparkling wave with azure wing,
Leaving their track in many a tiny ring.

And through the church-path, **still and sweet,**
    Where waving flowers their fragrance fling,
And rustling branches twine and meet
    O'er many a hidden spring,
The rustics wend their calm and peaceful way;—
Rest, thoughts of toil—it is **a holy day.**

His soft hand in his mother's prest,
    His merry eyes upraised to trace
The thoughts that, passing in her breast,
    Are shadowed in her face,
The young child boundeth on—the peigle rears
Its spangled head,—nor his light footstep **fears.**

THE VILLAGE SABBATH.

With shaking step, unsure and slow,
    And wasted form, and downcast eye,
Yet smiling on the groups that go
    So still and gently by,
The old man totters on — nor lonely he,
For children's children are around his knee.

They're gone — that young and happy throng —
    He hears no more the merry **tone**
Of their glad voices — and among
    The dead he stands alone;
And as he gazes round with swimming eyes,
Old and familiar faces round him rise.

But he shall hear **their voice no more**,
    Those old companions — the grass **waves**
Its dank and dewy tendrils o'er
    Their lone and silent graves,—
Whose very outline has worn faint and **dim**,
For many a year forgotten save by him.

No well-carved stone here rears its head —
    The cypress, like a funeral pall,
Waves its dark boughs above the dead,
    And they are nameless all ;
Yet mourn not thou — better than sculptured art
The monument of one fond human heart.

'Tis o'er — the hymn ascends to Heaven,
    "Glory to Him who died to save,"
Breathing of joy — of sins forgiven —
    Of hope beyond the grave,
They are not dead but sleeping — for the tomb
Is but the passage to a brighter home.

THE WANDERER.

She came—and none knew whence she came—
   Alone—that maiden meek and mild,
With her wan cheek, and fragile frame,
   And eye so dark and wild,
And noiseless step—as one of Spirit-birth
She seemed to glide upon—not tread the Earth.

She loved to wander 'neath the **shade**
   Of forest trees—and when we thought
To lure her hence, she, weeping, said,—
   "'**Twas** blessèd peace she sought:"
And 'twas her hapless lot to seek in vain
For that which she must never know again.

To haunt the beach when far on high
    The stars their holy watch did keep,
And peace was in the happy sky,
    And calm upon the Deep;
And all seemed fair, as at Creation's birth,
When sin was not, and Angels trod the Earth.

And still, and still she lingered nigh,
    When o'er the waves the tempest swept,
And the wild blast rushed pealing by
    As the forked lightnings leapt;
And when we gently strove her hence to bear,
She bowed her head, and murmured, " He is there."

And chanting low and mournful words,
    For days would haunt the dark green woods,
And listen to the song of birds
    In leafy solitudes,—
Or to the rippling of the stream, that bound
By mossy banks sent forth a silvery sound.

And when night's many voices rose,—
    Night's solemn voices soft and low,
Breathing of calm and sweet repose,
    That she might never know,—
Still kept beneath the cold and starlit sky
Her sleepless watch,— her Guardian — One on high.

She died—but not upon the bed
    Of weary pain : we laid her where
The parting sun a blessing shed,
    And the cool rushing air
Could sweep her brow, and trees around might wave,
That soon should sentinel her quiet grave.

Oh ! sad, yet beautiful decay !
    Though anxiously **we watched beside,**—
So gently did she pass away,
    We knew not when she died ;
But when we brake the silence long and deep,
We could not wake her from her dreamless sleep.

As when roused by some well-known strain,
    Old thoughts upon our hearts have rushed,
  (We deemed we ne'er might know again),
    We know not it is hushed,
Or when it ceased — but start to find it o'er,
And that each well-loved tone resounds no more.

We laid no stone upon her breast,
    But the dark sweeping willow flings
  Its shadow o'er her place of rest,
    And green and pleasant things
Around her wave, and children pause and tread,
With lowly reverence o'er her quiet bed.

THE OLD BARON.

A PROUD and stately mansion, half hid by grove and wood,
Time-worn and hoary grown with age, in ancient time there stood;
The grass was growing dankly round the hearth within its halls,
And the grey owls reared their nests in its ivy-mantled walls.

No sign, no trace of man was there—no voice—no human tone—
The bounding deer, the fearful hare: the Park was all their own—
All shy and timid creatures found refuge in its woods,
And birds sang all the day, from its leafy solitudes.

THE OLD BARON.

One solemn New Year's Eve, in the ancient Hall of state,
Alone in moody silence, an agèd man there sate,—
Sole Lord and Monarch he, of the world-forsaken place,
While round him hung the trophies of his proud departed race.

Stern effigies in mail stood threateningly around,
And tattered banners waving with a strange, unearthly sound—
Each in its old accustomed place, as in the days of yore,
But the slimy worm lay coiled on the damp untrodden floor.

A sound of bells came on the wind, from the little village near,
A glad rejoicing strain to hail the birth of the New Year,—
Type of the glorious peal, the grand triumphal chime,
That shall hail the deathless day, and sound the knell of Time.

The weight of ninety heavy years had bowed his lofty head,
His hoary locks like flakes of snow, around him waved and spread;
And many a furrow Age had traced upon his forehead high,
Yet had not dimmed the lustre of his proud commanding eye.

Still flashed its fires as they had done in former days of **pride**,
When foremost in the field he stood, his five brave sons beside;
When gallantly and proudly, he led them to the fight,
For valiant Rupert, good King Charles, old England, and the Right.

He saw them fall around **him, from the** proud and stately heir,
To the youngest one the **darling, with fair long flowing hair,**
But no cry came from his lips, **no tear bedimmed his eyes,**
"Not dead, not dead," the old man said, "the hero never **dies!**"

But from the world since that dark day he'd ever **lived apart,**
With all that weight of unshed tears upon his bursting heart;—
And now alone he sate, and mused upon the solemn past,
And Spirit-voices seemed to him to float upon the blast.

In thought he wandered back to his youth's bright scenes again—
He trod with her, **his** dear young bride, his noble broad domain;—
Sweet tones, like Fairy's whispers, seemed murmuring around,
And rustling trees, **and** hidden streams, sent forth a pleasant sound.

He felt her light and thrilling touch, he saw her gentle face,
He held her fondly clasped again in love's first warm embrace;
He heard her low and flute-like voice in tender accents speak,
And softly, as the summer's breath, her kiss fell on his cheek.

He saw her in her sorrow, in her meekness half divine,
Passing away like Autumn flowers, that die, and make no sign;
He held her mild and patient face upon his throbbing breast,
And watched her as she passed to her everlasting rest.

His little children thronged around to climb his knee again,
He heard their feet's low patter, like the fall of summer rain:
His first-born, with the features of his proud and ancient race;
His youngest, with its mother's eyes, and pensive angel face.

He saw them in their spring-tide, he saw them in their prime,
He saw them sleeping in their grave, he heard the death-bell chime;
He thought upon his waste of heart, the griefs of ninety years,
And fast, and fast, and bitterly, then fell the old man's tears.

The darkness passed, the glad morn rose all beautiful and clear,
And earth rang out a song of joy to hail the infant year;
But the long-pent heart had broken, there in his chair of state,
Enthroned, but rigid, dead, and cold, the stern old Baron sate.

THE TALE OF A SATIN GOWN.

The silvery stars were waning fast,
  Night closed her solemn sway,
Soft roseate clouds o'er the heavens were cast,
  And blent with the morning grey;—
When forth from her gilded couch of state,
  From the gay and brilliant ball,
Stepped one by the world called good and great,
  To her proud and princely hall.

Rare glittering gems in her locks were set,
    And flashed on her breast of snow,
The halo of triumph was o'er her yet,
    And brightened her fair young brow;
And a lustrous robe of peerless white,
    All wrought and broidered o'er
With twinkling stars of glancing light,
    On her stately form she wore.

And the Lady's eyes were dazzling bright,
    Glad smiles on her lip were seen,
And her heart beat high — that festive night
    Had a night of triumph been;
Sweet visions of love before her passed,
    As she sank on her couch of down,
And her last fond waking glance was cast
    On the beauteous satin gown.

Then a skeleton hand the curtain drew,
    And a shadowy form there stood,

And her heart's pulse stayed, for well she knew
 That it was not flesh and blood,—
But a pall-like robe around it flowed,
 And shrouded its fearful form,
That looming hung, like an awful cloud
 When fraught with a thunder-storm.

It beckoned her forth—that bony hand,
 She dared not disobey;
And the waning stars, a solemn band,
 Lit up their silent way:
On—on—through the broad and palaced street,
 The dismal alley, and lane,
Where the wide extremes for ever meet,
 Of Luxury and Pain.

And the ghosts of Pleasure flitted by,
 The Sisterhood of Sin,
With painted cheek and glittering eye
 That veiled the Grave within.—

Her scared eye looked on the living Dead,
    And saw thro' the borrowed bloom,
On the forehead's snow, and the cheek's deep **red**,
    A hand had written Doom.

She, shuddering, **saw before her rise**
    The realms of loom **and woe,**
Where skeleton shapes, with **hungry eyes,**
    Went hovering to and fro:
Dark homes, that never the sunshine knew,
    And human hearts **the same,**
Where all things hideous throve and grew,
    And gladness never came.

Children that never a childhood knew,
    That died a daily death,—
Dread haunts, whose pallid inmates drew
    A poison with every breath,—
Whose every day was this bitter strife,
    To hunger, thirst, and crave,

Who knew no hope in this weary life,
    And none beyond the grave.

It beckoned her on — that bony hand,
    She dared not disobey;
And the waning stars, a solemn band,
    Lit up their silent way:
Till she stood in a low and darkened room,
    Where the light of stars came not,
But a shadow, dense as of the tomb,
    Hung heavily o'er the spot.

And many a youthful form was there
    Around the midnight lamp,
With cheek grown hollow with toil and care,
    And brow all wan and damp;
All smileless was each lip and eye,
    No cheerful laugh went round;
But sharp and quick — incessantly,
    The needle's clinking sound.

But oh! what thoughts were in each **breast**
  Of the dear ones far away,—
Of blessèd haunts of peace and **rest**
  Where the quiet homestead lay!
The dewy hills, the green fields, where
  The peaceful cattle strayed,
The daisy-covered mead **so fair,**
  Where happy children **played.**

Some thought upon the churchyard green,
  On those who were at rest,
And almost wished themselves had been
  Within its tranquil **breast;**
Some prayed but once to feel **again**
  The soft **wind's** pleasant breath,
Then close their eyes **on** life **and pain,**
  And sleep the sleep of **Death.**

While some there were in this dismal band
  That never prayed or hoped,

Then the Spirit stretched forth its shadowy hand,
    And her spiritual eyes were oped;
The quivering light still beamed upon
    The busy and silent crowd,
But every shape was a skeleton,
    And stitching its own white shroud.

And ghastly forms still hovered there,
    Around each grisly frame,
Consumption wan, pale Want, Despair,
    And pallid cowering Shame;
While on the threshold, Sovereign meet
    Of all the Phantom Brood,
The earthworm trailing at his feet,
    The King of Terrors stood.

Then the Lady waked with a startled cry,
    And there in the moonbeams bright,
Lay the lustrous robe, all tranquilly,
    With its stars of glancing light—

The birds sang merrily in the sky,
To hail the glad morn's birth,
And the matin hymn rose pleasantly
From the rejoicing earth.

THE CHANT OF DEATH.

I am not of Earth — but Spirit-born —
   Yet the wide world owns my sway,
Its pomp and its might I laugh to scorn,
   For all must my Will obey. —
I visit the halls of dazzling light,
   Enter the loftiest domes —
And all is anguish and all is night,
   Where the King of Terrors comes.

I reign o'er the waves of the mighty Deep,
  I ride on the stormy wind—
On every shore where breakers **sweep**,
  My ruthless track you find:—
I soar on the wings of the pestilence—
  Am heard **on the tempest's crash**—
And when Earth **is veiled in gloom intense,**
  I sail on the lightning's flash.

Yet oft in loveliest guise I **dwell**—
  On the light of the clear blue **eye,**
On the blooming cheek set **I** my spell—
  They **wither—decay—and die;**—
And often I lurk **in the night-wind's sigh,**
  And steal in the youthful breast,
And gently—calmly—and silently,
  Doth that spirit sink **to rest.**

And I smile as I mark the youthful brow
  Bent over the midnight page,

And list the fond Enthusiast's vow
   At the shrine of bard and sage;
When I have doomed him to sure decay,—
   And known while his bays are green,
That his toilworn frame shall pass away
   From Earth—and be no more seen.

I care not for pomp or glittering crown—
   Serf and Lord are alike to me—
For the mightiest King must bow him down
   To a mightier King than he.
I speak, and the loftiest head must bend:
   From Creation's earliest dawn
I have reigned—and my reign shall only end
   With the last of woman-born.

All things of earth—of air—of sky—
   Must yield them unto me,
And the vast and glittering worlds on high
   Shall my parting conquest be;

For the Heavens shall melt and pass away
    Ere the work of Death be done,
And the Sun himself shall see decay,
    Ere my earthly race be run.

The Universe with my fame hath rung,
    Since my banner I unfurled,
And my parting requiem shall be sung
    'Mid the ruins of the world;
Lord over all with life and breath —
    The same triumphal chime
That sounds the dirge of the Monarch Death,
    Shall sound the knell of Time.

THE KING OF THE WORLD.

The loftiest throne may be o'ercast,
    The proudest pass away—
The mightiest spear must couch at last
    In rust and slow decay;
Kingdoms may sink 'neath the ebon pall,
    Of the shadowy past—what then?
Mine is a goodlier power than all,
    'Tis based on the hearts of men.

When Time was young, and the world **yet bare**,
    The stamp of its Maker God,
And the First Created, pure and fair,
    Its glad green surface trod;
While the morning-stars, all chaste and pale,
    Yet sang **o'er** the new-made **earth,**
The Spirits of Darkness cried, " All hail!"
    And Hell moved **at my birth.**

O'er the wide, wide world, my power is spread,
    Man — proud man, is **my** slave,
From his mother's breast to his last cold bed,
    From the cradle to the grave.
Wherever the golden sunbeams fall
    My dazzling front is seen,
From **the** Monarch's Court and Princely Hall,
    To the lowly churchyard green.

The churchyard — aye! — no priestly prayer,
    No solemn sacrifice,

O'er the silent Dead will echo there,
   'Till purchased with a price;
Oh! few are the words of hope and grace
   From the soul-redeeming word,
O'er the poor man's clay—prayers flow apace
   When my still small voice is heard.

Enter with reverence—softly tread
   The sacred House of Prayer,
Humbly and meekly—bow the head,
   All men are equal there!
Enter, thou man of tears and sighs,
   World-weary and grief-opprest,
" Come unto me," the Saviour cries,
   " And I will give you rest."

Enter, poor lost one—but not where
   Thy well-housed Brethren sit,
That Wealth should herd with haggard Care
   Is neither meet nor fit;

A mild voice preacheth brotherly love
   And charity — but I ken
That a mocking demon sits above,
   And scoffs at such holy men.

A young girl steps from her father's hall,
   But her brow is wan and sad,
Though fair sweet flowers before her fall,
   And all Nature seemeth glad;
With cheek as white as the sculptured stone,
   And lips all pallid and cold; —
Oh! a fearful sight to look upon
   Is the Bride that is bought and sold.

And not a pitying tear doth start
   O'er her dread and bitter lot,
None think of the crushed and withered heart,
   Of the worm that dieth not;
'Mid the clang of bells — the jest — the shout,
   She stands in her pride and sin,

Like a beautiful tomb all fair without,
    All ghastliness within.

There's a darkened room, where day by day
    A lone man worn and old,
With shrunken limbs, and locks of gray,
    Sits telling his heaps of gold;
With haggard cheek and glittering eye,
    Telling his heaps of gold,
Nor dreams that Life is fleeting by,
    As a passing tale that's told.

Little he recks of a shape of gloom
    That is tracking him on his way,
Of hearts that will dance o'er his unblest tomb,
    And leap o'er his senseless clay;
On his brow is graved man's doom — Decay —
    Yet he craves, and still will crave,
As though Human Life endured for aye,
    And Earth held not a grave.

Oh! the human heart may break, yet live—
  In the wet street, dark and cold,
A shivering woman waits to give
  Her more than Life for gold;
Black clouds o'er the angry Heaven are cast,
  And the whirring rain fast flies,
While round her scenes of the Awful Past,
  Like midnight ghosts, arise.

To me mild Charity bends the knee—
  The stern Truth boweth down—
And holy Justice looketh on me,
  And half forgets to frown.
Oh! talk not of the idolatry
  On the far-off Heathen Strand,
While a molten image is throned on high
  In every Christian land.

O'er the wide, wide world my power is spread,
  Man, proud man, is my slave,

From his mother's breast to his last cold bed,
    From the cradle to the grave.
Nations may sleep with the shadowy Past,
    Yet King of the World am I;
And my rule shall stand, and my reign shall last,
    Till Time himself shall die.

THE DRESSMAKER'S DREAM.

Long, long have Night's deep shadows spread
   Athwart the earth and sky,—
The pallid moon gleams **overhead,**
   The stars are out on high,
But Labour's day is not yet done,
The weary hands must still ply on
   Fast and unceasingly.

The very **air about her spread**
   With wan **disease** is rife,
More slender with each shortening **thread**
   Wears her own thread of Life;
The hectic flush upon the cheek,
The bright and glittering eyes bespeak
   How brief will be the strife.

Jaded and sleepless, worn and ill,
    She shapes a robe most fair,
But in the eyes of Heaven it will
    A blood-red aspect wear,—
Woven and wrought by starving men,
'Mid bursting hearts, hot tears, and then
    Fashioned by haggard care.

But sense and sight are failing fast,
    The present disappears—
Bright visions of the Dreamy Past,
    The ghosts of buried years,
Are rising round her—for awhile
Plays on her lips its old sweet smile,
    Forgotten are her tears.

She wanders by the rivulet,
    Thro' field and dewy vale—
Watered by many a sparkling jet,
    Bursts forth the primrose pale;
The modest daisies lift the head,
And like a sea of stars outspread
    Far over hill and dale.

She roams o'er sunny pasture-land,
    The sheep like snow-heaps seem,
The drowsy cattle brooding stand
    Midway in the cool stream,—
While stretched beside the bubbling springs
The lazy cow-boy sleeps — or **sings**
    Of many **a rustic theme.**

The soft air teems with pleasant sound,
    The woods are rife with song,
The ploughman on his homeward round
    Goes carolling along;
The tinkling brooklet winds its **way,**
The tiny cascades leap and play
    The mossy banks among.

A white cot peeping thro' **the trees** —
    It is her own dear Home,
E'en as she left it, now she sees,
    Ere she went forth to roam;
Lo, from the gate with joyous whoop
And welcoming shout, a goodly troop
    Of loving faces come.

The scene is changed—she stands once more
   Within that silent room,
More lonesome seems it than of yore,
   More sombre in its gloom;
The air like fire upon her falls,
The ceiling dark, the mouldering walls
   Enclose her like a tomb.

These cold damp walls they seem to move,
   They oscillate—they wave—
They hem her in—Oh! God of love,
   Father of mercy—save!
On, on they come without a sound—
They weigh her down—they close around
   One black and awful grave.

She starts—she wakes—the moonbeams bright
   Gleam thro' the lattice pane,
The voices of the holy Night
   Send up their solemn strain;
In Nature's calm she hath no part,
But turns with worn and aching heart
   To her sad toil again.

THE DEATH OF SCHILLER.

He waked from sleep — that gifted one,
  But o'er his brow and temples fair
Death's chill dews hung — a hand of bone
  Had stamped its impress there;
Gush, ye hot, bitter tears — fall fast as rain!
Ye cannot wash away that ghastly stain!

Men gazed in awe, and stayed the breath,
  Locked in the breast the half-heaved sigh,
All knew the spectral Monarch Death,
  The Spirit-King was nigh;
A nameless terror hovered o'er the spot,
They felt His presence, though they saw it not.

It was not dark, but o'er that room
    There hung a shadow dense as night,
'Till suddenly brake thro' the gloom
    A flood of silvery light;
The Poet saw it, raised his languid eye,
"Oh! once again," he cried, "then let me die."

Gently the Dreamer forth they bore,
    His long and last farewell to take,
For well deemed he that nevermore
    His eyes to Earth might wake.
Mutely he gazed, his weeping friends among,
Upon the glories he so oft had sung.

It was the peaceful twilight hour,
    The soft grey mists were rising fast,
The peasant's song was heard no more,
    The bird had sung its last.
Thro' the dim gathering shades slow stealing on,
The glittering stars looked forth all one by one.

DEATH OF SCHILLER.

Afar, on golden clouds reclined,
    The dying sun yet watched their birth,
And sadly, as from sister kind,
    Day parted from the earth.
The mild and pensive morn awaked from sleep,
On high her pure and holy watch to keep.

Meekly she glided thro' the Heaven,
    Looked on the Earth with looks of love,
And to the World awhile seemed given
    The calm of realms above;
Mountain and flowery plain, and rippling lake,
A purer, holier semblance seemed to take.

Earth saw it, and from cavern lone,
    From leafy grove, and waving wood,
From purling stream slow gliding on,
    From forest solitude,
From limpid brook, and dew-bespangled sod,
Sent up a song of blessing unto God.

DEATH OF SCHILLER.

And long the Poet gazed — his day
    Of hopes and fears was well-nigh past;
As snow beneath the sun's warm ray,
    His life was ebbing fast.
A little space — a few brief moments must
Give ashes unto ashes — dust to dust.

He, like that sun, must pass away,
    He, too, must sink in deepest night,
But to arise with brighter ray
    In glorious strength of light;
Darkness was round about him — but his eye
Pierced thro' its depths, and saw a cloudless sky.

They laid him on his pillow now,
    Leant on their breast his drooping head,
But still around his noble brow
    That silvery light was shed:
A long, cold shudder shook his wasted frame,
But o'er his parted lips a smile there came.

And blessèd deeds came back again,
  In Memory's sweet and tranquil guise,
As unto Earth in gentle rain
  The dews that from it **rise.**
Dear forms that he had loved in Life's young **day,**
Hovered around and beckoned him away.

"Calmer and calmer yet," he said,
  These were his dying words — his last;
Around them fell a sudden shade,
  The Angel by him passed.
And Earth of him owned nothing but a clod
Of stiffening clay — the soul had sought its God.

GO FORTH.

"Go forth!" so spake the bitter voice,
　"We will have none of thee,
A canker art thou, and a blight
　Upon Life's pleasant tree,
So moving full of misery,
　Where only joy should be.

"A shadow and a mystery
　Amid the bright and blest,
Thou comest like a dull nightmare
　Between us and our rest,
And we would fain the golden sun
　Should never seek the West."

GO FORTH.

So spake the World's harsh voice, nor I
   Had power to speak again,
For every word a poisoned barb
   Fell on my quickened brain,
And every feeling was absorbed
   In that keen sense of pain.

For I had **dearly** loved the **World,**
   And all its pleasant things,
And deeply had my spirit **quaffed**
   From Pleasure's sparkling springs,
And earthward-bound in rosy chains,
   My soul had furled its wings.

Oh, weary, weary change!—there fell
   Night's shadows **on** my day,
I trod **a** road without a goal,
   A white **and** dusty way,
And all around about me spread
   One everlasting **grey.**

All grey without—nor beam, **nor dews,**
   The leaden skies let fall,—

God's face was dark, I could not look
   Behind that awful pall,
And oh! the dreary life within
   Was greyer far than all.

One day it chanced—I know not how,—
   I sought a forest glade,
Where dusky elms and beeches tall,
   Such canopy had made;
The fern-grown sod was clothèd in
   Impenetrable shade.

Maybe, our Father, in His love,
   Took pity on His child,
That unseen Angels guided me
   Unto that forest wild;
And that it was their tears that fell
   In dews so sweet and mild.

As prone amid the ferns I lay
   Beneath a hoary tree,
Some holy influence abroad
   My deadened sense could see,

Almost it seemed a Mother's arms
  Were then embracing me.

Ah me! what dead and vanished years!
  What day-dreams past and o'er!
What ghostlike visions of my youth
  Came back to me once more,
As phantoms of the Wrecked that flit
  About the fatal shore!

But chiefly to my mind there rose
  A cottage trim and white,
Where twining rose and woodbine sweet,
  And jasmine—starry bright,
Such trellis o'er the lattice made,
  They almost barred the light;

And 'neath the shadow of the porch
  A woman pale and fair,
The mild Redeemer crucified
  Within her soul she bare:
You saw it in her holy eyes,
  Her meek and saintly air.

GO FORTH.

An old illumined Bible lay
  Wide open on her knee,
O'er which a golden-headed child
  Entrancèd seemed to be,
Tho' oftentimes his glance stole up
  That dearer face to see.

A flood of rich and mellow light
  Around the vision streamed,
A loving smile direct from God
  Unto my soul it seemed;
Nor of the sun — nor moon, but such
  As gladdens the Redeemed.

The soft wind like a Mother's kiss,
  The dropping dews like balm
Fell on my brow, — about me spread
  A deep and brooding calm;
No sound, save the low, solemn tones
  Of Nature's ceaseless psalm.

The light breeze stirred the circling boughs,
  I saw the purple skies;

A thousand white and gleaming stars,
    Like Angels' watchful eyes,
Looked down on me—then in mine own
    The tears began to rise.

My pale lips formed a prayer, God knows
    The words that they did speak,
It was such depth of bliss to feel
    Those tear-drops on my cheeks;
So strange the sense of joy—it left
    My spirit faint and weak.

God in the silence answered me,
    There was no voice, no tone,
But in my spirit's secret depths
    He made His presence known;
So Light upon my Night hath dawned,—
    I am no more alone.

THE TRIUMPH OF FAITH.

A VISION rose before mine eyes,
   Such ne'er may waking sight behold,—
No forms were they of human guise,
   No shapes of mortal mould,
But wild, and terrible, and dread—
Such as might haunt the drear death-bed
   Of sin, and crime untold:

No pleasant sun a blessing shed,
   No flowers sprang from the desert ground—
The Earth was thick with graves—the Dead
   Of ages were around;
Stupendous shapes its surface trod,
Yet left no impress on the sod,
   Their footsteps had no sound.

A dark and dreadful form was there,
   And from his bent and awful **head**
The streaming locks of hoary hair
   Were like a snow-storm spread—
A blight was in his breath **to chill,**
And change **all goodly things to ill**—
   Earth trembled at **his tread.**

The skies were starless, and his throne
   Was reared in darkness drear and vast—
The giant shades of Ages gone,
   O'er which had long been cast
Oblivion's veil and shapes of gloom,
Fresh from Corruption and the Tomb,
   Dread Shadows of the Past—

Thronged thickly round, and ever nigh,
   Yet still unseen around his path,
A form of gloomy Majesty,
   Such as the tempest hath.
I knew him by his fleshless brow—
His dart that strikes Creation low—
   Dark minister of wrath.

And one was there of mortal birth,
    With brow of thought and carriage high,
Fresh from our green and lovely Earth—
    A dauntless energy
Was in his step—the immortal soul,
That mocks the Grave and Death's control,
    Looked from his deep blue eye.

He faces that dread spectre now—
    He stands before that awful throne—
The Spirit's hand is on his brow,
    And yet, nor sigh, nor groan —
Some mighty, although unseen, power
Sustains him in this darksome hour,
    Though helpless and alone.

How changed! the bowed and tottering limb—
    The hollow cheek—the brow of care—
The sunk eye, lustreless and **dim** —
    The drooped head—all are there;
Beneath him **yawns** the ready tomb,
And yet he shrinks **not** from his doom,
    Nor yields him to despair.

He speaks — his words are calm **and low —**
    " I fear thee not, thou awful one, —
Although his mortal frame must bow
    Awhile before thy throne,
Yet vain thy power, and brief thy sway,
The deepest night still ushers day, —
    Then, Spirit, take thine own!

" Nor thine this dust — for it shall rise
    To join the starry hosts of them,
The ransomed spirits of the skies, —
    And thy last requiem
Ten thousand thousand human tongues
Shall chant — and Seraphs join their songs —
    Then where thy Diadem?

" I know that **Nature shall wax old —**
    That Heaven and Earth shall pass away —
The **mighty** Deep its depths unfold
    Merged in one vast decay.
That from the skies the stars shall fade —
But *Thou*, the ruin thou hast made,
    Dread King, shalt not survey.

"For in that hour thy knell shall sound,
  And all that e'er drew human breath,
From unknown graves, Earth's farthest bound —
  The giant seas beneath —
Shall wake to witness thy despair, —
Then where thy triumphs, Age? and where
  Thy victory — oh! Death?"

DEATH AT THE HALL.

LAST of his race!—last of his **race**!
   He sleeps within the Tomb,—
He sleeps within the narrow **grave**
   Enshrouded in its **gloom**:
His Mastiff fond, with bitter wail,
   Doth on his master call,
And desolation reigns within
   His old ancestral Hall.

That old pile echoed oft with song—
   Here Beauty did entrance
The mailèd heart of belted **knight,**
   With her bright magic glance;
While many a trophy proudly waved
   Around the oaken wall;
But now, each sound of joy is hushed
   In that deserted Hall.

Here light feet skimmed thro' mazy dance,
　　Here lip with lip did meet,
While honied words and soft looks made
　　Each moment yet more sweet:
Now all is changed—stern Death hath swept
　　Each form of light away,—
The very walls are ivy-grown,
　　And mouldering to decay.

The voice of woe alone is heard;
　　The peasant veils his face
And weeps for him, the kind old Lord,
　　Last of his goodly race:—
The beggar, too, with shivering limbs,
　　Outside doth vainly wait,
And looks with tearful eyes upon
　　The barred and gloomy gate.

No more the old man's kindly voice
　　Their drooping hearts may cheer,
Or from their heavy eyelids chase
　　The sad and bitter tear;
That gentle heart that warmed to all,
　　Alas! hath throbbed its last,
And he and all his pleasant deeds
　　Are numbered with the Past.

DEATH IN THE COTTAGE.

Tread lightly the threshold, and hallow the spot—
'Neath the low, humble roof of that desolate cot,
The Monarch of sorrow, in dreadful array,
With his army of Terrors asserteth his sway.

The soul of the peasant is loosened and free,
He is — as the Monarch of Empires must be,
When the pomp of this life shall have vanished away,
And its splendour be changed for the worm and decay.

The voice of his children is hushed at his gate,
And vacant and dreary the place where he sate;
The jasmine neglected trails over his door,—
And the home that once knew him, must know him no more.

Bright summer will come — but he may not behold it;
The corn-sheaf will rise — but he may not enfold it;
The crocus and blue-bell in beauty will wave —
But the heart that so loved them be cold in the grave.

The Old Village Churchyard must open again,
To receive the rude son of the hamlet and plain;
They have hollowed his bed where the sad willows weep,
In the lone, tranquil spot where his forefathers sleep.

But lovely and peaceful shall be his long rest,
Though no richly-wrought monument cumber his breast,
And hearts full of tenderness hither will come,
And shed their sad tears o'er the Peasant's last home.

OH! STRIKE THY HARP.

Oh! strike thy harp, and sing once more
    That old familiar strain;
It breathes to me of happy hours
    I ne'er may know again:
It tells of joys that long have fled,
    Of friends my youth hath known,
That from my side, like Autumn leaves,
    Have withered one by one.

It bringeth back old scenes to me,—
    My boyhood's happy home,
The cowslip-spangled fields, where I
    A child was wont to roam

The merry brook — the fountain lone —
   The sweet and leafy glade,
Where gushing springs, and hidden rills,
   Low music ever made.

I hear; and am again a child,—
   Mine eyes are full of tears,
And my worn spirit half forgets
   The griefs of after years!
Methinks such strains should sound thro' Heaven,
   When earthly sorrow o'er,
Long-parted friends shall meet again,
   And meet to part no more.

A VISION OF DEATH AND IMMORTALITY.

Night's sable shadows round me crept,
   Dim twilight o'er me spread,
There passed before me as I slept
   A vision wild and dread ;—
Strange, unknown realms I wandered o'er,
By human foot untrod before—
   The cities of the Dead.

I saw a vast and mighty plain
   Unbounded by a sky,
And my strained vision strove in vain
   Its limits to descry,—
Desert on desert—sea on sea—
World upon world, faint types might be
   Of that Immensity.

No flowers sprang from the arid sod—
  No soft dew on it shone—
It seemed a Land the blessèd God
  Had never smiled upon,—
There was no glorious sky above
To tell His Majesty and love,—
  Sun—starlight—was there none.

There was no sound of Life—no sound—
  Naught living but the worm—
That silence was so vast, profound,
  The motion of my form,
My footfall, thrilled my soul with fear;
They jarred—they smote upon the ear,
  As doth a sudden storm.

Black darkness, like a mighty pall,
  Hung o'er the ghastly scene,
So dense—the gloom that night we call
  As silvery light had been,—
Thousand on thousand years *that* night
Had been unbroken in its might,
  Nor dawning e'er had seen.

The Dead of Ages gone were **there,**
   And those of yesterday.
All who had ever breathed the air,
   And passed into Decay;—
Millions on millions—e'en the sod
Had drawn **the breath of** Life—I trod
   On human dust and clay.

The myriads that have died in fight,
   Unsepulchred were there,—
The crownèd head—the man of might—
   All festering and bare,—
And some on whom youth's **seal was set,**
Where fearful **beauty lingered yet,**
   E'en in corruption fair.

I saw in ghastliness arrayed,
   The Spectral Monarch stand,
Sharp, icy winds around **him played,**
   The sole in that dark land;
A fiery scroll his sceptre bore
Graved thus, "Till Time shall be no more,
   Almighty to command."

And round, in fearful order, stood
    The Princes of the Grave,
Fierce War—his right hand dripping blood,
    That still for blood must crave ;
And Fever gaunt, and wild Desire,
Consumed by an undying Fire,
    And restless as the wave.

Consumption wan, and wrinkled Care,
    The handmaids of the tomb,—
Pale Want, with bosom lean and bare,
    Where lay a thing of gloom.
A fearful shape, that issued thence,
Whose name was graven—" Pestilence,"
    In letters dark as Doom.

And then, methought, a solemn sound
    O'er that vast plain did ring,
The Spirits hovering around
    In chorus wild did sing
(Ne'er may such sound Earth's silence wake,
It was as though a tempest spake)
    The praises of their King.

" Lord of the Present — Future — Past,
   What Power is like to Thee?
Thou wast — Thou art — Thou still shall last
   Till Time shall cease to **be.**
Earth shall wax old — the heavens shall bow
Beneath the **weight of years** — but Thou
   The Death **of Time shalt see.**

" The mighty sun in gloom shall set —
   The skies shall pass away —
The moon her silvery light forget —
   The pallid stars their ray —
Tempest, and wind, and flood, shall cease,
And Ocean's rage be hushed to peace,
   Beneath thy mighty sway.

" Earth's farthest bounds thy **power proclaim,**
   Dread Lord of Life and Breath, —
The wide winds celebrate thy fame,
   The Ocean's unknown depth,
And untrod caves thy might declare —
Creation doth thy impress bear —
   Life is thy slave, — oh Death!"

Then suddenly, through that dense night,
    I saw a star arise,
A silvery star—like those that light
    Our own earth's mellow skies;
Ah God! what joy to me was given,
Oh! it was as a glimpse of Heaven
    Unto long sightless eyes!

And then, methought, "a still small voice"
    Rang o'er that vasty plain—
"Rejoice," it cried, "thou earth rejoice,
    Thy dead shall rise again!"
"Jesus, omnipotent to save,
Hath burst the Trammels of the Grave,
    And Death no more shall reign."

The Vision changed—Earth's thousand lands
    With hymns of praise did ring,
The mighty floods did clap their hands,
    The stars for joy did sing;
The mountains shook their hoary crown,
The ancient forests bowed them down,
    To hail the Saviour King!

THE BURIAL OF THE EMIGRANT.

As a party of emigrants was travelling through a beautiful and almost uninhabited country, one of the number, a young woman, recently married, sickened, and died, far away from any consecrated place of interment; her sorrowing friends selected for her last home a sweet and peaceful spot embosomed in trees, and left her there to sleep in undisturbed tranquillity till the last Trump shall bid the Dead awake. The following lines are supposed to express the feelings of the bereaved husband.

Lay her gently, lay her trustfully,
    Beneath her mother sod,—
Gone in faith and Christian meekness,
    To the bosom of her God.

Pure was she—as the snow-flakes,
    When falling to the earth;
Rich in all holy sympathies,
    That in the Heavens have birth.

She shone while yet among us,
    With the sweet and chastened light
Of a solitary star 'mid the
    Blackness of the night.

A happy calm breathed round her,
   Like that a pensive Even
Throws o'er the thoughtful spirit,
   Or a blessed dream of Heaven.

All was peacefulness about her,
   A sweet and quiet grace
Was in her every motion,
   Looked from her patient face.

Cross her hands in humble fashion,
   O'er her white and spotless breast,
Then leave her in her beauty,
   To her long untroubled rest.

Lay her gently, lay her trustfully,
   Beneath her mother sod,—
Gone in faith and Christian meekness,
   To the bosom of her God.

What though she must not sleep
   In the churchyard's hallowed shade,
Where the ashes of her Fathers
   In solemn trust are laid?

No priestly prayer hath risen,
  No sad and mournful bell
Hath tolled the work of Death,
  But the winds have rung her knell.

Glad sounds shall murmur round her,
  Bright flowers shall o'er her creep;
Soft Angel-eyes shall watch her,
  In her long and dreamless sleep.

For oh! there's something tells me,
  That a blessed Spirit keeps
A ceaseless watch around,
  Where the seed Eternal sleeps.

And sacred, though unconsecrate,
  In this lone solitude,
Since all Earth was Heaven-hallowed
  When God proclaimed it Good.

But oh! the bitter change!
  Oh! the blackness of this night!
Unbroken by a dawning,—
  By the promise of the light!

All is darkness in my mind,
    All is darkness in my brain,
Nought within me seems alive,
    Save the consciousness of pain.

Yet they tell me Spring is come,
    That the joyful Earth is drest
Like a fair Bride for her Bridegroom,
    In her rarest and her best:

That the green and dewy sod
    Is bright with early flowers,
Just awakened into life by the
    Sunny April showers:

That the voices, long so mute,
    From forest, hill, and grove,
Are singing as of old, of the
    Never-dying Love.

But oh! I hear them not —
    Nought can bid me now rejoice;
All the harmonies of Nature
    Are silent with her voice!

A FACT, 1847.

A woman sate in a joyless room,
  With walls all blank and bare —
Deep, and dense, and solemn its gloom,
  As though Hope ne'er entered there.
Her eye was hollow, her brow was sad,
  Her cheek was haggard and thin,
And every vein and bone she had
  Looked forth from her shrunken skin.

Thro' the rattling roof the wild wind whirred,
  It whistled around her form,
That shook as the forest leaves when stirred
  By the passing of a storm.
She pressed her hand on her clammy brow,
  As her white lips moved in prayer,
But a colder, ghastlier hand, I trow,
  Had stamped its impress there.

A presence was there lips pale to breathe,—
    The spectral King of kings—
He hovered so nigh she sate beneath
    The shade of his mighty wings;
A veil all dark as a vanished age
    Betwixt her and the world was cast,—
The Future to her an unwritten page,
    And a sealèd book the Past.

Dear tones, long hushed with the voiceless dead,
    Seemed sadly murmuring round,
E'en her own light and muffled tread
    Had a strange, unwonted sound.
In the flickering light the rafters tall
    Had a dim and spectral look,
And the very shadows on the wall
    A ghostly semblance took.

One glance she cast o'er the dreadful past,
    Since her life of toil began,
And the scalding tears fell thick and fast
    Through her fingers worn and wan;—
She thought of the boards so richly spread,
    The homes of the great and grand,
While she must die for the lack of bread,
    In a so-called Christian land.

No sister kind, no mother was by,
    No fond and loving breast,
Whereon she might breathe her parting sigh,
    And pass to her long last rest.
O'er her shuddering frame Death's darkness fell,
    Yet no Priest was by her side,
In the words of faith and hope to tell
    That a Saviour, too, hath died.

The earthworm lurked in her thin robe's fall,
    A shroud in its **every** wave;
The ceiling above her seemed **a pall**,
    And the floor beneath a grave;
In a shivering heap she bowed her **down**
    (Think of it, man, in thy pride),
In hunger, and dirt, and cold,—alone—
    As a dog that Christian died!

They have laid her low in her narrow bed
    'Neath the green earth's quiet breast,
But the pauper living, or pauper dead,
    Hath here no place of rest!
To the rich—the great—the proud by birth,
    The soil belongeth, alone,
The poor hath not, on the whole wide earth,
    E'en a grave to call his own.

They have muttered prayers, and laid her where
  The dark weed foully creeps,
But no daisy-covered mound is there
  To mark where a sister sleeps;
They have laid her low — but a voice shall rise
  From that cold and darksome sod,—
That shall pierce the earth — shall pierce the skies,
  To the Throne of the Living God.

CHRISTIAN CHARITY.

Fair the maiden was and slender
  As the lily newly born,
Chaste her glances were, yet tender
  As the glimmer of the dawn:
Wheresoe'er those glances lighted
  Darksome objects changed their hue;
Drooping blossoms, seared and blighted,
  Opened lovely to the view.

Gentle was her voice, and holy,
  Softly fell it on the ear,
As the streamlet rippling slowly
  When the summer heat is near;
And her motion was in keeping,
  Noiselessly she seemed to pass,
As the playful shadow sweeping
  O'er the long and glossy grass.

White her robe as mists of morning
   Clinging round an Alpine height,
All her bosom's meek adorning
   One fair cross of liquid light;
Snowy flowers sprang in her honour
   Where her light feet touched the strand,
All God's angels smiled upon her,
   As she trod the pleasant land.

But the pure and pious maiden,
   She of more than mortal birth,
Wandered, sad and heavy-laden,
   Outcast on the thankless earth,—
Fiercely from the palace driven,
   Chased from e'en the lowly shed,
She, the child — the loved of Heaven,
   Found no spot to rest her head.

Strong in love, though bowed by weakness
   (Like her Master all Divine),
Blessed she them, and then in meekness
   Sought the Church's hallowed shrine.
Golden sunlight softly streaming
   Through each richly painted pane,
Rainbow colours, sweetly gleaming,
   Robed in glory all the fane.

CHRISTIAN CHARITY.

Glad Hosannahs, high ascending,
    Round the fretted roof they rang;
Children's voices with them blending,
    Of the world's Redeemer sang;
All earth's weary ones, who sadly
    Yearned for peace and tranquil rest,
Thronged its portals,—with them gladly,
    She, with cross upon her breast.

Never seemed her hope to falter,
    All her sorrows mildly borne,
'Till from out each incensed altar,
    Hidden demons laughed in scorn;
Then her spirit died within her,
    And she bowed her holy head,—
Ah, who back to earth shall win her?—
    Christian Charity hath fled!

www.ingramcontent.com/pod-product-compliance
Lightning Source LLC
Chambersburg PA
CBHW020309170426
43202CB00008B/558